DAD'S
BABY

Throughout the book we have referred to the child as "he" or "him" – obviously we do so only for convenience. Similarly, we often refer to the "parent" – by which we mean either the mother or father or any other person who may be acting, either temporarily or permanently, in a parental role.

DAD'S BABY

Everything a Father Needs to Know About Looking After a Baby

The Diagram Group

CORGI BOOKS

DAD'S BABY

A CORGI BOOK 0552 12742 6

First publication in Great Britain

PRINTING HISTORY

Corgi edition published 1986

Copyright © 1986 Diagram Visual Information Ltd.

This book is set in 9/11pt Baskerville

Corgi Books are published by Transworld Publishers Ltd.,
61–63 Uxbridge Road, Ealing, London W5 5SA, in Australia
by Transworld Publishers (Aust.) Pty. Ltd., 26 Harley
Crescent, Condell Park, NSW 2200, and in New Zealand by
Transworld Publishers (N.Z.) Ltd., Cnr. Moselle and
Waipareira Avenues, Henderson, Auckland.

Printed and bound in Great Britain by
Cox & Wyman Ltd, Reading

The nature of information on the methods of caring for and
feeding babies and infants is often the subject of interpretation.
While the greatest effort has been made to ensure the accuracy
and completeness of the information presented the reader is
advised that no claim can be made that all the relevant
information concerning the care and feeding of babies and
infants is included in this book. The reader is advised to consult
his medical practitioner for information concerning the
treatment of any medical condition. Corgi Books cannot be
held responsible for error or for any consequences arising from
the use of information contained herein.

Foreword

Fathers, after some years in eclipse, are now becoming
fashionable again. Not all of them insist on being present at the
birth of their child: indeed, some mothers do not welcome this.
But many men seem at last to have realised that bringing up a
child can be a sentence of sixteen years' hard labour for a
mother. They are also beginning to realise that helping with
feeding, nappy-changing and pram-pushing is not only
interesting and rewarding in its own right, but does not
necessarily damage their reputation as red-blooded males! In
addition, help offered with tact and careful timing can convert
a harassed, short-tempered mother into the sweet girl she once
was. Dad's Baby is an owner's manual as vital to your life as
the one in the glove pocket of the family car. With it, you
should only need your GP when you really cannot find the
answer, and you should be able to hold your own in the
presence of even the most knowing of elderly female relatives.
Go to it!

Dr. Geoffrey Smerdon
M.A.(Oxon), B.M., B.Ch., M.F.O.M.(R.C.P.)

CONTENTS

Section 1:
PRACTICAL
CHILD CARE

Section 2:
FEEDING

Section 1
PRACTICAL CHILD CARE
Introduction

Responsibility for the day-to-day care of babies and young children has traditionally belonged to the mother, but more and more couples are discovering the advantages of a more equal sharing of many aspects of practical child care. Many modern fathers now know that taking an active part in the daily care of their children can be one of the most rewarding and enjoyable aspects of family life.

This first section of the book provides a wealth of useful information on everyday infant care. Included is advice on holding and handling the baby, coping with crying, nappy changing and toilet training, signs of illness, bathing and dressing babies and children, equipping the nursery, travelling with the baby, routines for babies and small children, and information on sleeping patterns and bedtimes.

Certain aspects of your baby's care may always be a problem: he may hate bathtime, bedtime, being dressed, or being put down for a nap. These problem areas will require extra attention, and so of course will illness or lack of appetite. But armed with this small book, the inexperienced father will soon gain the knowledge and confidence needed to make a major contribution to the daily care of his young child.

coping with the new baby

A new baby – and particularly a first baby – brings many changes to the lives of both parents. For some, the joy of having a new member of the family more than compensates for any loss of personal freedom. But many others find that it takes some time to get used to the need to adjust their life styles to take into account the requirements of a new and demanding baby. Sometimes the situation is aggravated by the mother suffering from a period of postpartum depression (thought to be caused by hormonal changes in a woman's body after childbirth), or by the father feeling that his partner has no time to spare for him. Lack of sleep frequently makes matters worse. Considerable understanding is called for on both sides of the partnership of parenthood, and a father who helps with the practical aspects of looking after his child will find that all the family benefits.

New fathers and mothers alike commonly experience feelings of anxiety about their ability to cope with their baby's demands. A major difficulty at first is that you and your partner will be unfamiliar with the baby's behaviour patterns. In time you will learn what to expect, but in the meanwhile the baby will make his needs known by crying. Specific aspects of care such as feeding, changing, and bathing may seem problematic to begin with, but they will soon become second nature. Babies do not ask for total sacrifice – only for love, food, and warmth.

In the beginning you will have help from your health visitor who will call on you, without you asking her, about ten days after the birth. She is a trained nurse, and will tell you about your nearest Child Health Clinic which you can visit at regular times each week.

equipment for the baby

Preparations for the arrival of a new baby include the assembly of a wide range of equipment. This is best done quite early in the pregnancy, when the expectant mother is able to get about easily. Shopping trips made with your partner will not only help her a great deal, but can be enjoyable for you both. Before rushing into buying a lot of expensive new equipment it may be worth asking around your friends to see if anyone can lend you items such as a cot or pram. Another way of saving money is to buy used equipment, but do remember that any repainting must be done with leadfree paint.

equipment checklist

A selection of possible items:
1 Teats
2 Bottles
3 Sterilizing tank
4 Teat jar
5 Measuring jug
6 Knife
7 Measuring scoop
8 Bottle brush
9 Sterilizer
10 Jug
11 Baby bath
12 Soap and dish
13 Two bowls
14 Bath thermometer
15 Two facecloths
16 Towels

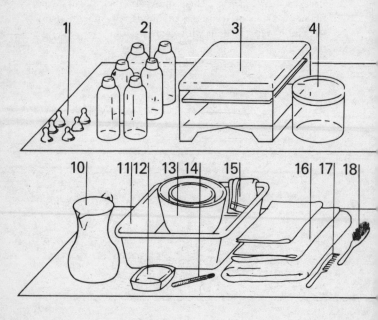

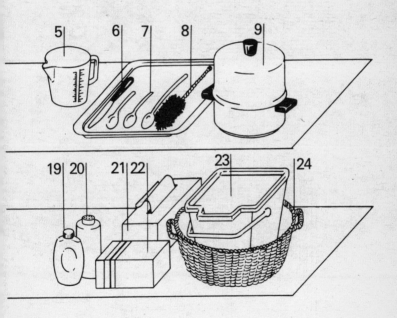

equipment checklist (continued)

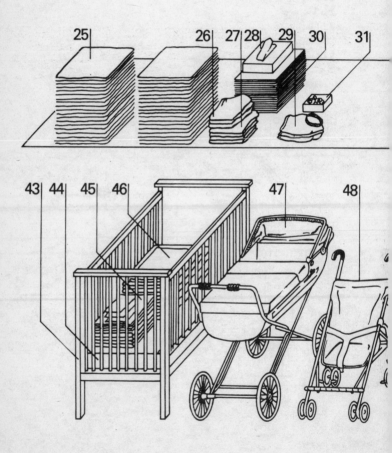

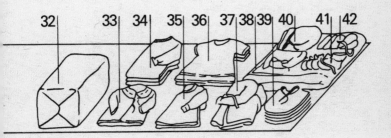

| 32 | 33 | 34 | 35 | 36 | 37 | 38 | 39 | 40 | 41 | 42 |

25 Cotton towelling nappies
26 Vests
27 Nightgowns
28 Disposable nappy liners
29 Waterproof pants
30 Muslin nappy liners
31 Nappy safety pins
32 Disposable nappies
33 Cardigans
34 Stretch suits
35 Sweaters
36 Dresses
37 Coat

38 Baby blanket
39 Bibs
40 Bonnets
41 Mittens
42 Bootees
43 Cot
44 Mattress with waterproof cover
45 Sheets
46 Blankets and cot cover
47 Pram
48 Baby buggy (not for a young baby)

early routine

The diagram shows a typical routine for a young baby taking six feeds a day. In the early weeks, a baby's day consists almost exclusively of sleeping and feeding periods; the exact timing of the schedule is usually determined by the baby waking when ready for the next feed. (See Section 2 of this book for detailed information on feeding your child.)

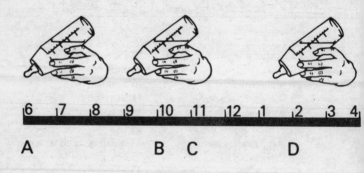

A 6 a.m. – feed, nappy change, sleep
B 10 a.m. – wash or bath, feed, nappy change
C 11 a.m. – sleep, outside or in
D 2 p.m. – feed, nappy change, sleep
E 5 p.m. – active time
F 6 p.m. – wash or bath, feed, nappy change
G 10 p.m. – feed, nappy change, sleep
H 2 a.m. – feed, nappy change, sleep

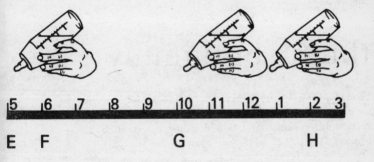

5   6   7   8   9   10   11   12   1   2   3

E   F   G   H

physical contact

A reliable and continuous loving relationship experienced from birth on provides the baby with a firm basis for future development. Research suggests that close physical contact, and not food, is the most important factor in the formation of the baby's first emotional attachments.

Babies like to be held in close body contact – being particularly happy in positions that simulate clinging – and a reassuring cuddle, from the father just as much as from the mother, will often work wonders when a child is upset.

Aids such as carry cots and prams may be a blessing to parents, but if used to excess they can deprive the baby of valuable physical contact. A baby sling worn in front or on a frame on the back and carried by either parent can be a useful alternative.

thumb or dummy

Young babies have an instinctive need to suck, and many like to suck their thumbs in addition to sucking during feeds. Thumb sucking may continue later, by which time it is essentially a comforting device.

Only if thumb sucking continues after a child has his adult teeth is there a risk of permanent damage – and by this time even the most enthusiastic thumb sucker is likely to have given up the habit.

Some parents prefer their baby to suck a pacifier or dummy, and it does seem to be easier for a child to abandon his dummy than to give up sucking his thumb.

If a dummy is used it must be kept scrupulously clean – and never dipped in tooth-decaying sweet substances.

handling the baby

Handling the baby may seem a daunting prospect, especially to the new father. In practice, however, most people soon master all the procedures they will need.

When lifting or carrying a young baby it is important to support his neck to prevent it from jerking back; supporting the neck with your hand or arm is all that is needed to prevent an alarming shock reaction.

The baby is likely to be startled if he is picked up suddenly, especially if he is unaware of the handler's approach. Talking to him as you approach him will remove the element of surprise. Illustrated overleaf are two basic handling techniques – one method for turning and lifting the baby, and another for raising him to a sitting position.

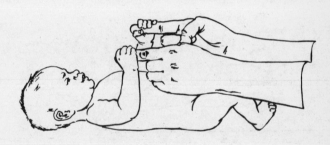

turning and lifting the baby

1 Grip the upper part of the baby's body.

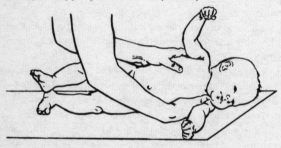

2 Turn the baby slightly to one side.

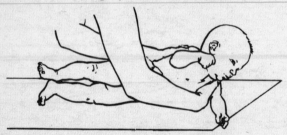

3 Using your free arm, reach through the baby's legs and lift him up, supporting his head with the other hand.

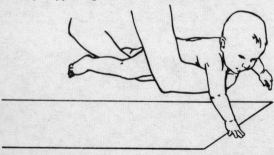

raising to a sitting position

4 Grip the baby by his upper arms and shoulders.

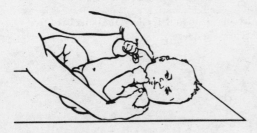

5 Turn the baby to rest against your arm.

6 Supporting the baby's head, raise him to a sitting position.

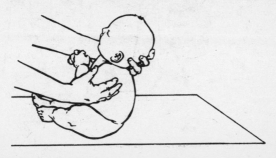

21

carrying the baby

Illustrated here are four ways of holding and carrying the baby.

1 A traditional 'comforting' position with the baby's head against the adult's shoulder.
2 A forward-carrying position that allows the older baby free movement of his arms and legs.

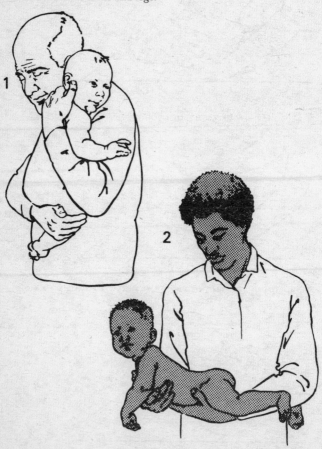

3 Hip-carrying position – a good way of carrying an older baby who can control his head movements.
4 Baby sling – also for an older baby who can hold his head up – gives everyone mobility.

cold and heat

It is possible for a baby, from birth, to regulate his body temperature in response to changes in temperature around him. But the body mechanisms that allow him to do this are still inefficient.

Cold is generally more of a problem for babies than heat. A baby who is inadequately dressed in a cold environment needs a lot of energy to keep himself warm. A baby who has become chilled normally responds to the cold by using energy to create additional body heat – but he is unable to store this heat, and so is forced to continue his efforts until relieved by outside warmth.

Serious problems can occur if the air temperature drops suddenly and markedly when the baby is asleep. It seems that a baby's temperature control mechanisms start to function only when he is almost awake. A controlled bedroom temperature, and a sleeping bag are therefore strongly recommended.

If the baby has become chilled it is important to get him warm before adding clothing.– otherwise the extra clothing will merely keep in the cold. If the chilled baby is lethargic, with reduced respiration and pulse rates, medical attention should be sought at once.

Heat High environmental temperatures are less likely to cause serious problems than low ones. A baby will soon cry if he is too hot – and the problem is easily identifiable. Removing a layer of clothing, wiping away the perspiration, and perhaps a drink of water are usually all that are needed to restore his comfort.

fresh air and sun

Babies and children generally benefit from spending part of the day outdoors.

Fresh air improves the appetite, brings colour to the cheeks, and probably reduces the risk of infection by preventing the air passages from becoming too dry.

It is normally quite safe for even a young baby to be taken outside in his pram – provided that he is suitably dressed, well sheltered from the wind, shaded from the sun, and that there is no fog. Most older children enjoy a daily walk or a period of outdoor play.

Babies and children have sensitive skin that burns easily, and care must be taken to avoid sunburn by using sun lotions. A very short sunbathe – two minutes maximum on the first day – can be beneficial. A light hat when the sun is hot is a must even for older children.

coping with crying

Crying is the most direct way a young baby can communicate;
if he cries it may be an indication that something is wrong.
Babies have characteristic ways of crying depending on what is
troubling them, and most parents soon learn to distinguish
between cries for different reasons.

Normally the causes of crying are straightforward, and once
they have been dealt with the crying soon stops. Frequent
causes include hunger, wind, teething, general discomfort,
boredom and loneliness. Crying may also be caused by
disturbing a child to undress or change him. A baby crying for
no apparent reason is probably only asking to be cuddled.

Some reasons for crying are, however, more difficult to remedy.
Notable among these is colic, which is painful for the baby and
distressing for the parents.

Another difficult problem is that of dealing with what are sometimes called 'hypertonic' babies. These babies are particularly tense, and start at even the slightest noise or handling. Many suffer from colic, or are prone to long periods of irritable crying. In time a hypertonic baby will calm down, but for the first few months it is best to disturb his sleep as little as possible.

If crying is in any way unusual, particularly persistent, or if the child appears in any way unwell, medical advice should be sought without delay.

Once you and your partner have become accustomed to your baby's behaviour patterns, you should find that coping with crying becomes much easier.

Coping with crying (continued)

1 Colic is a severe abdominal pain that recurs daily in some babies between the ages of two weeks and three months. It is notoriously difficult to treat (see p. 114).
2 Hunger will make the baby cry. A baby who has taken insufficient milk at a feed typically wakes after about an hour and cries for another feed.

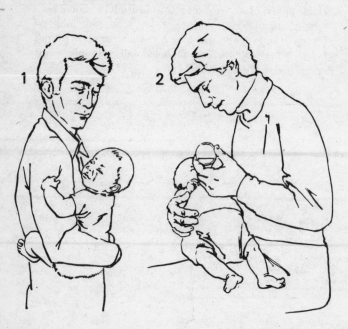

3 Teething begins at different times in different babies, but most have a miserable time. A doctor may give special pain-killers in severe cases.

4 Illness may make the baby cry. A doctor should be called if the baby looks or behaves unusually, vomits (see p. 113), has a raised temperature, or is drowsy.

5 Loneliness Babies cry for attention and love. They need to be cuddled and cannot be 'spoiled' in the first months of life (see p. 18).

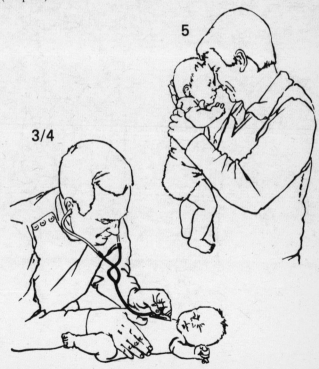

5

3/4

coping with crying (continued)

6 Discomfort causes babies to cry. The baby should be dressed in light clothes, and kept in a warm, draught-free room away from noises and bright lights.

7 Wind is often relieved by cuddling the baby over the shoulder (see p. 108). Vigorous back-slapping is rarely effective.

8 Wet nappies do not seem to worry most babies, unless they have nappy rash (see p. 38).

9 Hypertonic babies are unusually irritable and difficult to manage. A doctor will sometimes prescribe a mild sedative.

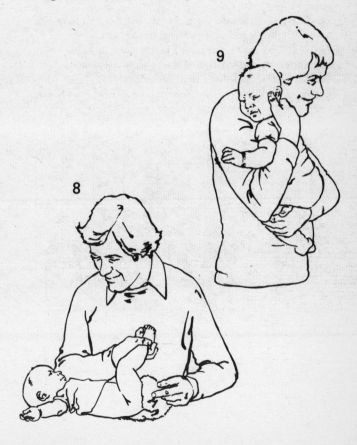

nappies

Many new fathers show great trepidation over changing
nappies – but the technique is easily learned.

Various styles of nappies are currently available. Traditional
terry towelling nappies are usually square, but other shapes
can also be bought. To make washing easier many people
favour using muslin or disposable liners along with towelling
outer nappies.

Plastic pants are usually worn over the nappies, but should be
avoided if the baby is suffering from nappy rash.

Disposable nappies either have a plastic outer lining, or are
worn under specially designed plastic pants. Although
comparatively expensive, disposable nappies are often
preferred by people who are short of time or away from home.

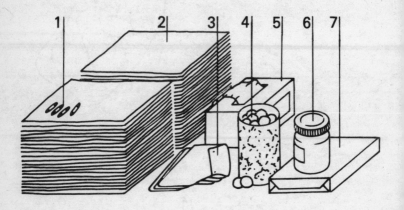

1 Towelling nappies and pins
2 Muslin liners
3 Pants for disposable nappies
4 Cotton wool for cleansing
5 Tissues
6 Baby lotion or cream
7 Disposable nappy liners
8 Disposable nappies
9 Baby powder
10 Waterproof pants for towelling nappies
11 Nappy pail

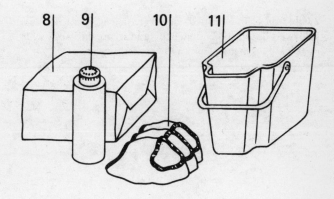

folding a nappy

Illustrated opposite are three popular ways of folding the usual square nappy.

1 Triangular fold Fold the nappy into a triangle and fasten the three corners with a single pin. (For detailed instructions see p. 36.)

2 Kite fold Fold in the two sides to give a long, pointed shape. Fold over the top and bottom flaps, and secure the nappy with two pins. This method gives a thicker centre panel.

3 Triple fold Fold over one-third of the nappy and then fold the rectangle into three. Fasten the nappy with two pins. The extra thickness should go at the back for girls and in front for boys.

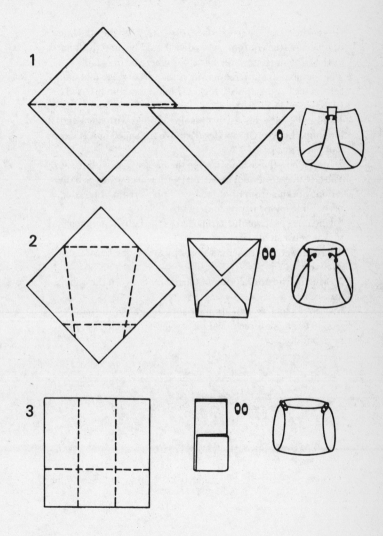

changing a nappy

It is useful to have a flat surface on which to change the baby's nappies. All the equipment needed should be directly at hand as the baby must never be left alone where he may fall.

The method illustrated opposite is for a triangular-fold nappy but stages 1 and 2 apply whichever folding method is used. (Also see p. 34.)

1 Raise the baby's body by grasping his legs with one hand, the forefinger between his ankles. Remove the soiled or wet nappy and place in a pail.

2 After a bowel movement, wipe the nappy area with tissues. Wash with cotton wool moistened with warm water or baby lotion, working from front to back. Apply cream or powder, if used. Slide folded nappy under baby.

3 Fold one corner of the nappy across the baby's stomach and tuck it between his legs.

4 Lay the second corner of the nappy across the baby's stomach.

5 Bring up the third corner of the nappy between the baby's legs.

6 With the fingers beneath the nappy to protect the baby's stomach, pin all three thicknesses together, placing the pin horizontally.

cleaning nappies

The traditional method of cleaning nappies is by washing. The stools are first scraped from the nappy into the toilet and then the nappy is rinsed and washed in very hot, soapy water. Nappies should also be boiled for a few minutes to sterilize them.

The task of cleaning nappies has been made easier with the development of special sterilizing products. In this method the nappy is scraped clean, immersed in a cold sterilizing solution in a plastic pail for two or more hours, and then rinsed several times in clean water.

Nappies are ideally dried in the sun or in an automatic drier; both methods destroy many bacteria.

Many people now decide to use labour-saving disposable nappies or liners.

nappy rash

Nappy rash – patches of redness and spots in the nappy area – is a cause of great discomfort.

It can result from sensitivity to soap, bleaches or sterilizing solution, or fabric rinses used on the nappies; from powders or lotions used directly on the skin; or from irritation caused by wet or dirty nappies. In older babies, it is usually caused by the reaction of the skin to ammonia formed by the interaction of stools with urea in the urine.

To treat the condition: boil nappies for 10 minutes and rinse with an antiseptic rinse; try using one-way liners or disposable nappies; change the nappies as frequently as possible; do not use waterproof pants; use a cream on the nappy area; and expose the area to the air as often as possible.

normal stools

The stools (bowel movements) of babies vary in appearance and frequency according to age and method of feeding.

During the first two or three days of life a baby normally passes 'meconium stools' which are sticky and green-black in colour. These stools consist of the waste products that accumulated in the intestines during the last weeks before delivery. For many babies, the first of these stools is grey in colour and is called the 'meconium plug'.

As the baby adapts to milk feeds the stools become green-brown and are known as 'changing stools'. When milk feeds are established the stools become mustard yellow. The transition from 'changing stools' can take just a few days or as long as four weeks.

The frequency of passing stools can vary enormously. Some breast-fed babies produce stools after every feed during the first few months; others produce as many as 15 daily. Bottle-fed babies tend to produce fewer stools at this time – usually between one and four a day.

In general the stools of a breast-fed baby are softer and less well formed than those of a bottle-fed baby.

As they grow older, both breast-fed and bottle-fed babies tend to produce stools less frequently.

Breast-fed babies in particular are likely to have very irregular bowel movements at times; an interval of seven days between stools is not rare, but the doctor should be called if the baby appears unwell.

problems with stools

Diarrhoea in infants is a serious complaint that needs medical attention. Sudden onset is usually a result of infection. Gradual onset can be a result of careless milk formula mixing – too much sugar is often responsible – or the introduction of a new substance to the diet.

Constipation is most common in bottle-fed babies. Stools are hard and difficult to pass. Adding brown sugar or maltose to milk formula can help. Laxatives should only be given on medical advice.

Blood in the stools of newborn babies results from swallowing maternal blood at delivery. Streaks can result from fissure in anus caused by constipation. Large quantities indicate a serious disorder needing urgent medical attention.

Stools of unusual colour can result from the introduction of any new substance to the diet. Bulky grey stools result from over-concentrated formula mix. Black stools can be caused by medicinal iron prescribed for anaemia.

daily routine

A regular daily routine can make life easier for parents, and
help give a young baby a valuable sense of security. In addition,
performing the same set of actions every day can give
confidence to the new father and mother in the first weeks after
the baby's birth.

In the early months, the routine will be largely dictated by the
baby's physical demands. These demands, and their timing,
may vary slightly from day to day and it is important that the
routine should be flexible enough to accommodate them. It is
not, for instance, essential to bathe a baby at the same time
each day, nor is it necessary to change his nappies before each
feed if his hunger seems to outweigh his discomfort. (A typical
daily routine for a young baby is given on pp. 16/17.)

After the first few months the daily routine for the baby will
become more varied. The number of fixed points in the day
decreases, as less of the infant's time is spent asleep or feeding.
By 12 months a baby is typically taking three meals a day and
having a nap in the morning and afternoon.

During the next few years much of both parents' time and
energy will be spent in guiding the child's early exploration of
the world about him. It can be an exhausting time, especially if
it is accompanied by the addition of a new baby to the family. A
day with some degree of structure is recommended throughout
the pre-school years. Careful planning will make life easier for
all the family; children will know what to expect, and you and
your partner should gain time to pursue your own interests.

bathing the baby

A bath is part of most babies' daily routine, and many fathers enjoy this aspect of caring for their children. Baths are usually given just before either the mid-morning or the early-evening feed. Many parents who are unable to get home soon enough to bathe their children on weekday evenings will find that they like to take over weekend or holiday bathtimes.

On these two pages we show equipment needed for an all-over wash or 'sponge bath' (see pp. 46/47) or a basin bath (see pp. 48/49). Included in the illustration are items used during the bath itself, and also towels, a clean nappy, and fresh clothing for after the bath. A bath thermometer is useful if it provides reassurance, but the old-fashioned elbow test (see p. 44) is just as effective.

1 Basin
2 Jugs of hot water
3 Soap in dish
4 Cotton wool
5 Facecloth
6 Cotton-tipped sticks
7 Bath towel
8 Baby lotion or oil
9 Baby powder
10 Baby shampoo
11 Safety pins
12 Bath thermometer
13 Clean clothes
14 Nappy
15 Bottle for after the bath
16 Baby bath
17 Waterproof bath apron

bathing procedures

Most new babies can be given a basin bath (see p. 48), but a sponge bath (see p. 46) is sometimes recommended for the first few weeks. Many of the procedures are similar whichever type of bath is to be given.

Before you begin, make sure that the room is warm, that you have washed your hands, and that all the necessary items of equipment (pp. 42-43) have been gathered together. It is also extremely important to check that the baby's bathwater is neither too hot nor too cold. Water of the correct temperature (95-100°F, 35-38°C) will feel comfortable if you dip your elbow into it; alternatively you can use a bath thermometer if you have one.

Before starting the actual bath, you may wish to clean the baby's nose or ears (very carefully, see p. 50) or to wash his hair (see p. 45). It is also usual to wash the baby's face at this stage. Never use soap on a baby's face; just wipe it very gently with a facecloth or cotton wool dipped in warm water.

Always keep a firm hold on the baby while you wash him. This may seem difficult at first, but you will soon learn what to do. Most important of all, never ever leave a baby unattended in the bath – even for a moment.

hair care

Washing A young baby's hair and scalp should be washed with gentle soap or shampoo up to three times a week, and with warm water at other bathtimes. The baby's head should be supported over the tub or basin, as shown below. Care must be taken to rinse the head carefully if soap or shampoo is used. An older baby need not have his scalp rinsed so often, but should have his hair washed regularly.

'Cradle cap' This is a yellowish, waxy crust that commonly forms on the scalps of babies at the age of about six weeks. It should be treated by massaging the scalp with baby oil before washing the hair.

Brushes and combs Only use good-quality, soft brushes and combs, and take care not to tug the hair when removing tangles.

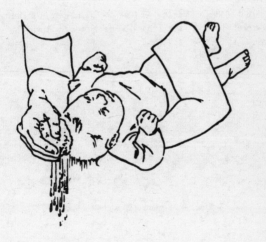

sponge bath

On these two pages we give a step-by-step guide for giving your baby a sponge bath.

1 With the baby on his back, take off all his clothes above the waist. Then apply soap to his neck, chest, arms, and hands, paying special attention to all skin folds and creases. Now carefully rinse off the soap with clean, warm water, and pat him dry with a soft towel. Next unpin his nappy but do not remove it.

2 Carefully turn the baby on to his front, supporting his neck with one of your hands. Apply soap to his back and, lowering the nappy, also to his buttocks. As before, pay attention to all skin folds and creases. Rinse off all the soap with clean, warm water, and pat the baby dry with the towel.

3 Return the baby to his back, and remove his nappy. Now wash his abdomen, being very gentle with his navel. Finally wash, rinse, and dry the baby's legs, feet, and genitals, being very careful always to use a front-to-back movement in the genital area.

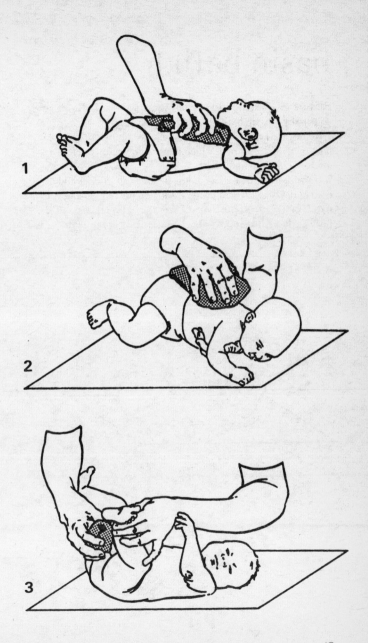

47

basin bath

Here we give a step-by-step guide for a basin bath. Never give your baby a basin bath just after feeding him.

1 Remove the baby's clothes, leaving his nappy until last. He is now ready to be soaped, which may be done either before or after placing him in his bath.

2 If the baby is to be soaped outside the bath, this should be done quickly to prevent lather drying on his skin. Using your hands or a cloth, apply soap all over the baby's trunk and limbs. Always use front-to-back movements in the genital area.

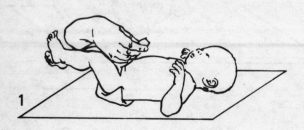

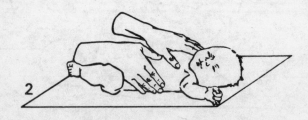

3 Now lower the baby into the basin, holding him as shown in the illustration, with his back and neck supported by your arm, his far arm held by one of your hands, and his ankles grasped (with forefinger between them) by your other hand. Once he is sitting in the basin, release his ankles and use that hand to soap or rinse him. Make sure you keep a firm hold on him with your other hand, and continue to support his head and back.

4 Once he is thoroughly rinsed, lift him out of the water and pat him dry with a soft towel. Take particular care to dry properly around the navel and wherever the skin is folded. If you wish, you can end by applying baby powder, lotion, or cream.

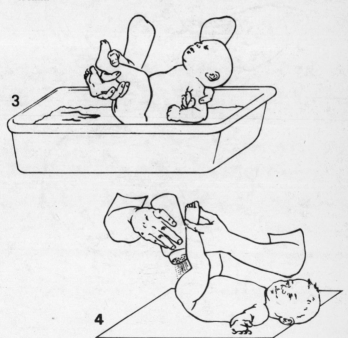

ear and nose care

A baby's ears and nose are very delicate and should be cleaned only when they are very dirty or clogged. Use moistened cotton wool swabs or cotton-tipped sticks and clean only the outer areas. Never poke into a baby's nose or ears or you may cause serious damage.

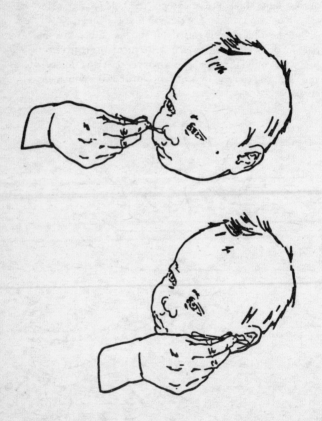

nail care

If the baby's nails are dirty they can be cleaned with the blunt end of a toothpick.
If his nails need trimming, use blunt-ended scissors to cut them, preferably when he is asleep.

dressing the baby

Babies grow quickly so careful planning is needed when organizing baby clothes. Seasonal requirements vary and should be remembered when selecting baby clothes of different sizes.

Garments should be easy to launder and dry, and preferably need no ironing. Deeper colours look fresher longer than traditional pastel shades.

Dressing the baby is simplified if clothes have few buttons or frills. Lacy-knit or fluffy garments are best avoided as the baby may inhale some of the fibre.

Simple nightgowns that tie at the back, and one-piece stretch suits are most suitable for the baby's early days (see p. 15).

A Cardigan Gather sleeve into loop with one hand; with the same hand grasp the baby's hand and draw arm down through sleeve (**1**); rock or lift baby on to other side (**2**) and ease the cardigan around the baby's neck; draw other arm down through sleeve as described.

B Pullover Gather pullover into loop; slip opening over back of head then forward over front, stretching over forehead and nose.

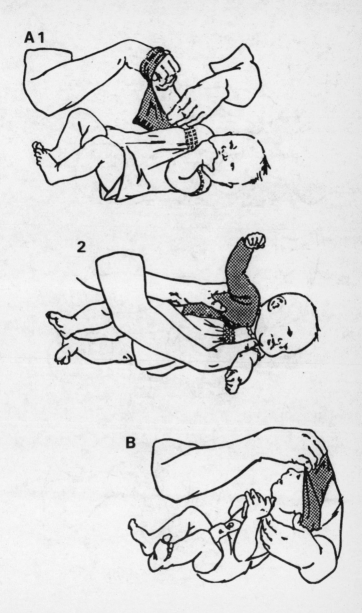

53

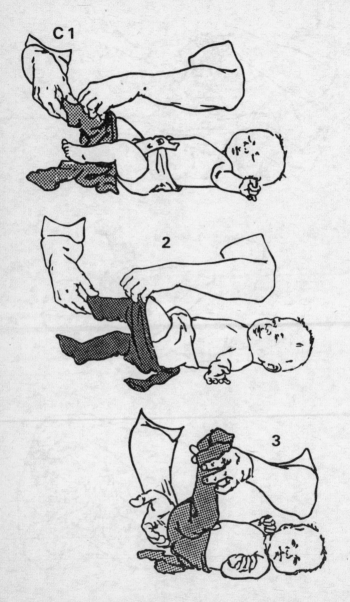

dressing the baby (continued)

C Stretch suit Gather one leg of the suit into a loop and ease the baby's foot and leg into it (**1**); gather second leg of suit into loop and ease baby's other leg into it (**2**); grasp baby's ankles; raise baby's legs and ease suit up to waist (**3**); put on top of suit in same way as cardigan.

care of the baby's feet

A baby's feet are soft and pliable and easily distorted. In the early months, damage can be caused by bedclothes tucked too tightly around the feet when the baby is lying on its back.
It is important to check that socks and the feet of stretch suits are big enough to allow free movement. Soft shoes for non-walking babies are best avoided as they may hinder the normal development of the feet.
A baby learning to walk should go barefoot as much as possible.

types of crib or cot

The baby will spend much of his time asleep, so all the equipment must be both safe and comfortable. In the early months, many babies sleep in a crib (**1**), cradle or carry cot on a stand (**2**). These have enclosed sides which reduce the risk of chilling from drafts. When buying a full-size cot (**3**) there are several points to consider. It should be sturdily built with vertical bars no more than 2½in (6.5cm) apart, and a safe latch on the side that can be raised or lowered. The mattress, either foam or horsehair, should have a waterproof cover. A pillow is not recommended for the first year. Fitted sheets are time-saving and easy to use. Blankets should be light, warm, and easy to launder; acrylic fibre is a good choice.

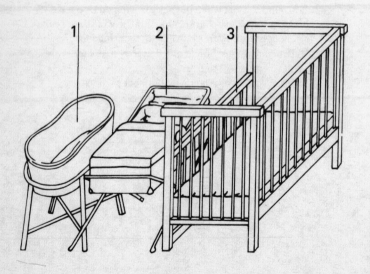

equipping the nursery

The crib or cot is the only essential item of equipment in a nursery. A flat surface for nappy changing and a storage unit for baby clothes and equipment, however, are strongly recommended. Also useful is a comfortable nursing chair for feeding.

A number of safety and health factors need consideration. Walls and furniture should be painted with leadless paint. Curtains and blinds should be made of flameproof fabric. Flooring should be easy to clean and non-slip. Scatter rugs may cause a serious fall.

The room should be kept warm – not lower than 65°F (18°C) – and the crib should be placed in a draught-free position.

1 Changing surface
2 Storage unit
3 Nursing chair
4 Cot

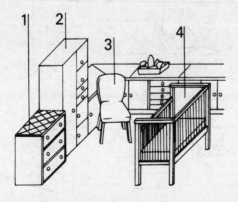

baby's sleepwear

A simple cotton nightgown (**1**) is the traditional sleepwear for
young babies. Many people, however, now favour dressing
their babies in easy-to-wash terry cloth stretch suits (**2**). As
babies become more active and are likely to kick off their cot
covers it is a good idea to use a sleeping bag or all-in-one
sleepsuit (**3**).

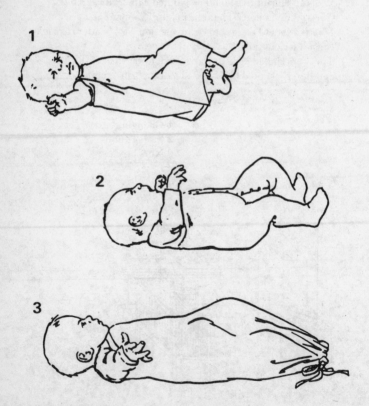

sleeping positions

For the first three months a baby sleeps in the position in which he is placed. The front position (**1**) is sometimes recommended as any regurgitated feed can easily trickle out of his mouth. The back position (**2**) allows the baby to look around when he wakes. Only when he is about six months old can a baby sleep unsupported on his side (**3**); a younger baby can be kept in a side sleeping position by supporting his back with a rolled towel or sheet.

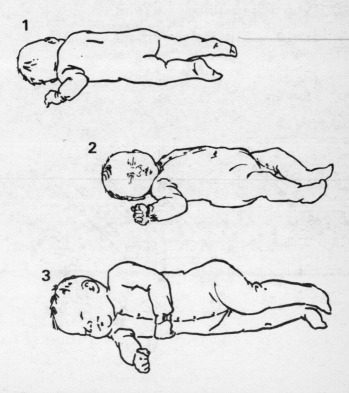

travelling with the baby

Trips with a baby should always be carefully planned: it is important that the baby's normal routine remains unchanged as far as possible. A good idea is to carry in a large bag all the equipment needed for feeding and caring for the infant. A damp facecloth, a towel, and tissues are useful for children of all ages. Given here is a list of suggested equipment for comfortable travel.

1 Carry cot and restraining straps
2 Nappies, possibly disposable
3 Prepared feeds
4 Dummy
5 Baby food
6 Tissues
7 Extra garments
8 Damp facecloth and towel in plastic bags
9 Toys
10 Potty

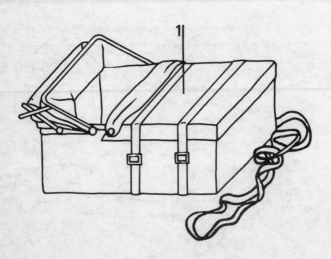

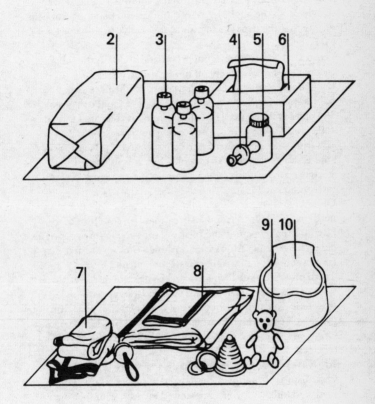

trouble-free travel

Undertaking any journey with young children can present problems for the adults in charge, but careful planning can help ensure that the trip is as safe and comfortable as possible for everyone.

Car travel Safety is most important and children should be secured on the rear seat at all times. Young babies can travel in their carriers held by restraining straps on the back seat. Older babies should travel in special seats attached to the rear seat and older children need junior seat belts. If you can, fit childproof locks to the back doors of your car.

Car trips with a baby need particularly careful thought. Very young babies generally sleep while the car is in motion, and stops need to be made only for feeding and changing. Keep all the equipment you need at hand (see pp. 60/61).

Older babies who remain awake for at least some of the trip need toys to play with, and an occasional piece of fruit or a biscuit. Frequent stops and plenty of distractions are needed for older children too. Always allow enough time on a trip to stop for a visit to the toilet, a short walk, or a picnic.

Train or bus travel If you can make your trip midweek the train or bus is less likely to be crowded. Reserve seats and, if travelling overnight, try to arrange a sleeper. This gives you a private place in which to attend to the baby. In addition, many large stations have a special room where babies can be fed and changed.

Air travel First, be prepared for delays before take-off. Have fresh disposable nappies, changing equipment, extra clothing, food, and milk with you – not stowed away in your luggage in the aeroplane hold. Most airlines are very helpful to adults travelling with children, especially if you warn them in advance. Check with your travel agent or airline office which facilities they offer before you leave.

Aeroplane take-off and landing can be alarming for a young child. A baby can be given a bottle of cooled, boiled water, and an older child a sweet; sucking helps equalize the pressure in the ears.

Boat travel Most boats offer the same kind of facilities as airlines. Again, check before your departure. Do remember the particular hazards on board ship; ensure that your children are supervised at all times.

Entertaining your children On trains, aeroplanes, and boats, reading books, drawing books, and games are ideal, though they may cause headache or sickness in a car. Games like 'I spy' and popular counting and guessing games, singing and reciting nursery rhymes are enjoyable diversions for children of any age. Very young children will usually appreciate a familiar toy.

Motion sickness Before a trip never show concern if your child is susceptible to motion sickness. Give him plain food and water only, and carry close by you a supply of plastic bags, a damp facecloth, a towel, and a change of clothing. Anti-sickness pills taken in advance can also help ensure a comfortable trip.

getting dressed

From the age of about two, most children show an interest in dressing themselves. By school age, most children can manage all but the most difficult fastenings. It is sensible to encourage independence by providing simple clothes such as those shown here.

1 Simple hair style
2 Tee shirt
3 Jacket with easy-fastening strip
4 Elastic-waisted skirt
5 Thick tights (or socks)

6 Buckle-fasten shoes
7 Simple hair style
8 Sweater without fastenings
9 Elastic-waisted trousers
10 Elastic-sided shoes

toilet training

The paragraphs below describe a typical pattern of pot training, but obviously there will be considerable individual variations.

Some babies are put on the pot from a very early age in the hope of 'catching' urine or stools. It is now generally agreed, however, that true toilet training cannot begin until the child is getting near the age at which he is physically able to control his bladder and bowels.

Between 15 and 18 months some children give a signal that the nappy has been wetted or soiled. This should be encouraged and most children then progress quickly to indicate that a bowel movement or urine is imminent. At this stage, notification and the action of the bowels or bladder may be simultaneous so that on many occasions it is too late to get the child to the pot in time. Nevertheless, praise should still be given. Later the child will be sufficiently familiar with the sensations of emptying his bladder or bowels to give plenty of warning on most occasions.

Some young children are frightened of falling from the toilet seat, or by the sound of the flush, and should always be accompanied by an adult or older child. Graduating to the toilet from a pot can be made easier if a special infant seat is used.

There will be accidents – especially with urine – when the child is tired, ill, or excited. But no reprimand should be given.

Night dryness is hardest to achieve, although taking the child to the toilet or potty at around 10 p.m. can often prevent wet bedclothes in the morning.

toilet training equipment

The most basic item of equipment used during training is a pot. Most are made of plastic and some have a shield that makes them suitable for both girls and boys. It is important to wash and sterilize the pot thoroughly after each use.

Training pants – made of towelling with a waterproof backing – are useful in the early stages of training. Later a special seat and step for the adult toilet may be used. Some infants prefer a commode chair.

1 Training pants
2 Pot
3 Commode chair
4 Toilet seat
5 Toilet step

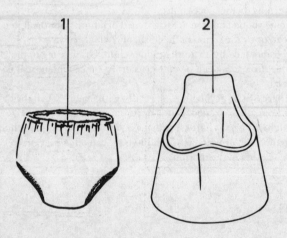

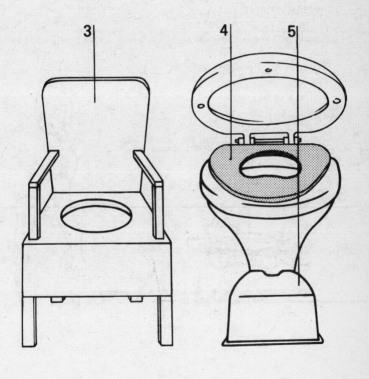

67

stages in training

Children go through the stages of toilet training in a particular sequence but the timing varies from child to child.

A No control
B Notifies after bowel movement or urination
C Notifies too late
D Usually notifies in time for bowel movement
E Usually notifies in time for urination. Clean during the day
F Dry during the day
G Clean day and night
H Dry day and night

year

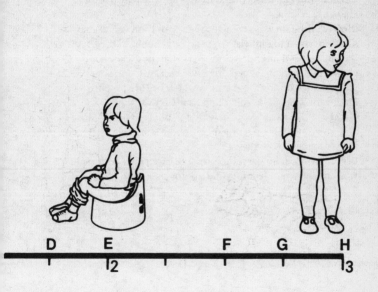

D   E   F   G   H

2   3

children's clothes

Many factors affect the choice of clothes for children. In general, clothes should be selected that are appropriate to a child's varying activities.

Clothes for play should be hard wearing, in an easy-to-clean fabric, and preferably dark in colour. Constant nagging about getting dirty is bad for all the family. It is much better to dress your child in clothes that need little attention.

School clothes should be easy for the child to manage by himself; unnecessarily difficult fastenings should be avoided. This is particularly important on days when the child's timetable includes sporting activities for which he has to change his clothes.

'Best' clothes are worn comparatively rarely and since they are soon outgrown it is unwise to spend large sums on them. At certain ages some children have very definite ideas about clothes and fashion. When this is the case, you and your partner must decide the extent to which you are prepared, or financially able, to let your child have his own way.

Hand-me-downs are extremely useful, but to avoid jealousy and resentment, younger members of the family should receive at least some new clothes.

Clothes will last longer if they are well cared for – with regular washing, prompt mending, and appropriate storage.

children's shoes

The fit of children's shoes matters much more than their appearance. Children's feet grow quickly and should be measured regularly for width and length with the special gauges used in shoe shops.

The structure of shoes is also important. The soles should be flexible to allow a springy step. The uppers should be supple where the toe joints bend but firmer in the arch for support. Shoes that fasten with adjustable straps or laces are recommended as they hold the foot at the back of the shoe and prevent it from slipping forwards and cramping the toes. Though it is important to keep the feet dry in wet weather, it is unwise to wear rubber boots for long periods, as they restrict the evaporation of sweat.

routine at one year

Illustrated here is an outline routine for a one-year-old. Rigid adherence to a routine is unrealistic for most families but a measure of planning makes life easier for everyone. If you are usually out of the house all day, try to build in a regular time each day when you can be with your infant.

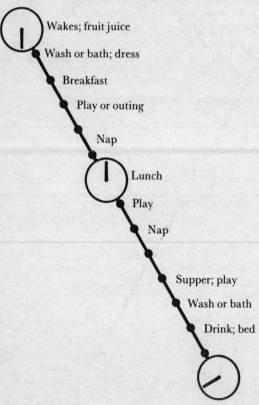

Wakes; fruit juice

Wash or bath; dress

Breakfast

Play or outing

Nap

Lunch

Play

Nap

Supper; play

Wash or bath

Drink; bed

routine at three years

At three years, most children are very active but still tire easily. A nap, or at least a quiet time in his room, is to be encouraged, and bedtime should be quite early.

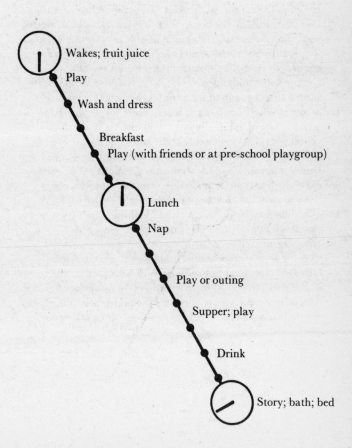

Wakes; fruit juice

Play

Wash and dress

Breakfast

Play (with friends or at pre-school playgroup)

Lunch

Nap

Play or outing

Supper; play

Drink

Story; bath; bed

school-age routine

A child's daily routine changes radically when he first starts attending school, and most children need a good deal of parental support to help them in this new situation (see opposite page). A school-age child spends much of his day away from home, but a fair amount of planning is still required. In the morning different members of the family must try to co-ordinate their times of waking, using the bathroom, eating breakfast, and leaving home. Schoolchildren should be given a nourishing breakfast, and should be able to eat it unhurriedly. Preparation for school should also be relaxed and it helps if any equipment needed is organized the previous evening.

Getting your child to school on time is your responsibility. Be sure to allow enough time for the journey whether you are accompanying him or not; it is very unsettling for a child to arrive at school habitually late. Similarly it is important to collect your child punctually at the end of the day. If you occasionally make different arrangements for his collection, do ensure that your child knows in advance. Even if your child is old enough to return home alone, ensuring that someone is there to greet him will increase his sense of security.

The child may be given schoolwork to do at home. Try to see that this is done – providing a quiet place and a little encouragement if necessary.

Evening activities and eating times vary a great deal from home to home. Each family must work out a pattern that suits it, and children should learn from an early age the need to fit in with other people's plans. Bedtime should be early enough to ensure that the child is not tired at school the following day.

starting school

Starting school is one of the most important events in a child's life. Some children look forward to going to school and enjoy it from the first day. Many others, however, have some difficulty in settling down. During their first weeks it is quite common for children to display some signs of strain. They may be generally irritable and ready to cry; they may have nightmares; they may return to thumb-sucking or begin nail-biting; or they may return to bed-wetting. This is normally a short phase; if it persists beyond the first few weeks the child's teacher should be consulted.

There are several ways in which parents can prepare a child for school life.

As early as possible in his life, your child should be encouraged to take an interest in a wide variety of topics. You and your partner can help by talking to him, reading him stories, and by taking time to answer his questions with care. Ensure that he is familiar with basic school equipment – pencils, paper, books, and paints. Teach your child to dress and undress himself, to go to the toilet unaided, to listen to and carry out simple instructions, and to recognize his own possessions. Make sure, also, that he knows the basic rules of road safety.

Playing with other children outside his own home helps accustom a child to being separated from his parents, and visiting the school before he becomes a full-time pupil is invaluable if it can be arranged. Otherwise, taking him past the gate or school playground when the children are out playing may help alleviate some of his anxieties.

how much sleep?

Individual sleep needs vary enormously. Some young babies sleep as much as 80% of the time, while others seem to be wakeful from birth. Children and adults, too, appear to have very different personal sleep requirements. In general, however, sleep needs decrease with age. An indication of sleep needs at different ages is given here in the diagram (based on the findings of H. P. Roffwarg, J. N. Muzio, and W. C. Dement). Researchers have discovered that there are two basic types of sleep: light, or REM, sleep (when rapid eye movements can be observed), and deep, or NREM, sleep (without rapid eye movements). In older children and adults, dreams are most likely to occur during REM sleep. In infants, REM sleep is thought to be not necessarily related to dreaming.

Shown opposite are the typical sleep needs and types of sleep at different ages.

Hours awake
REM sleep
NREM sleep

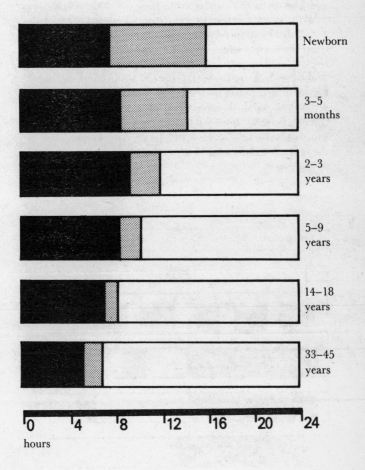

Newborn

3–5 months

2–3 years

5–9 years

14–18 years

33–45 years

0   4   8   12   16   20   24
hours

sleeping patterns

The distribution of sleep during a 24-hour period changes with age. The young baby will typically have five or six sleep periods a day, waking when hungry and sleeping when fed. As the baby gets older he will spend more of the time awake, with sleep concentrated into a long night sleep and a number of daytime naps.

A two-nap-a-day pattern is usually established in the second half of the first year. This is followed, usually early in the second year, by a one-nap-a-day pattern which persists throughout early childhood. From about age four children usually sleep only at night, with total sleep needs decreasing as they get older. Shown below are typical sleep patterns at different ages.

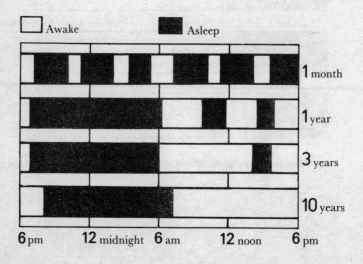

bedtime routine

The establishment of a regular bedtime routine can be
comforting and reassuring for a young child, and may help
prevent the formation of any serious sleeping problems.

The period before bed should be as calm as possible. It is a time
when working fathers and mothers are often able to play an
active part in the care of their children. Playing a game with a
parent out at work all day, or sharing a story, can often be a
highlight for a child who spends most of the day with the other
parent or someone else.

You can also encourage your child to take part in his own
preparation for bed. He can turn on the bath taps (under
supervision), undress himself, help dry himself, and put on his
nightclothes. The pre-bed routine should be tackled with an air
of certainty and inevitability. In this way the child will quickly
learn that he cannot successfully delay bedtime by discussion,
argument, or pleading.

A certain amount of bedtime ritual is necessary for most
children. Many insist on having a toy or doll in bed with them;
such objects give a child a valuable sense of security when he is
left alone. Others may ask for a drink or an extra kiss. As long
as the bedtime requests remain reasonable it is probably
sensible to grant them. Do, however, guard against the
development of long and complicated rituals; they are most
likely to be a delaying tactic.

refusing to sleep

Almost every child goes through phases of refusing to settle
down when put to bed. There are a number of reasons for this.
Childhood is interspersed with countless new experiences, and
at bedtime the child may simply be too excited to sleep.
Children, like adults, need a little time to unwind before sleep
comes easily.

The young child's growing enjoyment of the company of others
can sometimes make him reluctant to leave the family in the
evening, and this unwillingness may be reinforced by
interesting noises from elsewhere in the home.

Alternatively, he may simply not be tired. Afternoon naps
continued too long or taken too late in the day may lead to
problems at bedtime. Adjusting the daily routine as the child
gets older should put matters right.

Sometimes the child's refusal to settle down is due to anxiety or
a genuine fear of being left alone in the dark. Reassurance,
together with a familiar toy, a nightlight, or leaving the
bedroom door open and another light on should help the phase
to pass more quickly.

Some toddlers refuse to lie down in their cots at bedtime. They
should be left sitting or standing; they can be covered later.

Many children habitually cry when left at night. In most cases
this is merely a 'testing' cry and if it is ignored the child usually
drifts to sleep quite quickly. More persistent bedtime crying is a
greater problem, and in severe cases a doctor may prescribe a
sedative to help re-establish the habit of falling asleep.

early waking

Many children regularly wake very early in the morning. This is perfectly normal but can cause an unwelcome disturbance especially in the case of a young child who is at his brightest and most sociable after a night's rest.

It is often possible to encourage a young child to play quietly in his bed in the morning until a more reasonable hour; a mobile to watch or toys to play with may delay the disturbance for a valuable few minutes.

In some cases, a 'bribe' of a drink or a biscuit set out the previous night may also be useful.

Older children can be taught not to make too much noise until a particular signal – for instance, the ringing of an alarm clock. Sharing a room may also help solve the problem as the children may amuse one another and play quietly until a reasonable hour.

Section 2
FEEDING

Introduction

A baby's chief requirements – and pleasures – in life are food, physical contact, and warmth. When he is being fed he receives all three and establishes a close bond with the person who is providing the food. A new father may feel that he will be unable to share in this bonding process. This need not be the case; there are many ways in which a father as well as a mother can respond to a baby's needs.

This is particularly easy if the baby is bottle-fed. The father can obviously do all the things for his baby that the mother can – prepare and give the feeds, hold the baby close, and provide warmth and affection.

If the baby is breast-fed, many fathers feel isolated and helpless; in fact, there are many ways in which the father can share in the feeding process. He can fetch the hungry baby, 'burp' or wind him, change him, and return him to his crib or cradle when the feed is over. Most important, however, is the reassurance, support, and encouragement that a father can give to a breast-feeding mother. Breast feeding can be a tiring and lonely affair, and simply providing companionship can make the difference between success and failure, enjoyment and resentment.

In this section of the book we show the new father many of the practical aspects of feeding. The advice covers the preparation of the milk, giving a feed, methods of winding the baby, and the process of weaning the baby on to solid foods.

As you become increasingly familiar with your own baby, you will learn to distinguish between the different types of cry. This individual knowledge of your child will prove your most valuable asset in meeting his physical needs.

demand or schedule?

Experts used to recommend a strict four-hour feeding schedule. At present, however, a more flexible approach is generally in favour – with many babies now being fed on a self-demand basis. Most babies, whether fed on schedule or demand, have dropped the late-night sixth feed by eight weeks.

Schedule
The most common timetable for a schedule-fed baby receiving five feeds a day (top).

Demand
A typical self-demand pattern for an eight-week-old baby on five feeds a day (bottom).

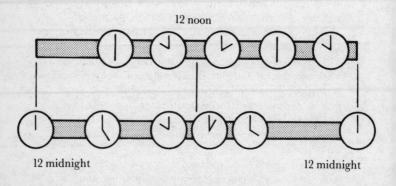

12 noon

12 midnight   12 midnight

feeding the baby

The physical contact with another person that feeding the baby automatically entails – whether by breast or bottle – is vital for a baby's well-being. During a feed, always hold and cuddle the baby and be as relaxed as possible. In this way a warm and intimate relationship can develop.

Where a choice is possible, more and more women are choosing to breast feed their babies, and most doctors welcome this as they regard it as the safest and most natural method of infant feeding. Some experienced fathers promote it too: it can be very satisfying to watch a mother suckle her baby and there is no need to mix formula or sterilize bottles.

However, if you are an inexperienced father you may feel that you have nothing to offer, and worry that you may be excluded from this important and rewarding aspect of your baby's care. This need not be the case. There are many ways of becoming involved which will strengthen the father's bond with his child and may also enrich his relationship with his partner.

Many new mothers are naturally anxious about breast feeding. They may doubt their ability, especially in the earliest days when an unco-operative baby may refuse to suck competently. They may think that their milk is insufficient or of poor quality. A positive interest, and continual encouragement, praise, and reassurance from the father is invaluable at times like these.

At feeding time you can demonstrate your care for the baby by taking the hungry infant to his mother, and afterwards by winding him.

On some occasions the breast-fed baby may need to be given a bottle and this is a good opportunity for the father who wishes to hold and feed the baby himself.

Changing the nappy, bathing the baby, and putting the baby to bed may be done equally well by either parent. Your help in these tasks will relieve the pressure on the mother as well as strengthen the bond between you and your child.

breast or bottle?
breast feeding

Quality The constituents of breast milk are present in near perfect proportions for the baby's optimum growth and development throughout the breast-feeding period.
Colostrum, secreted by the mother in the first few days after the birth, is rich in antibodies and gives valuable protection against some gastric infections.
Breast-fed babies are less likely to suffer from nappy rash, and are less likely to be overweight.

Quantity Only by test weighing is it possible to tell how much milk has been taken at a feed. Milk supply generally adjusts itself to cope with the baby's demands, but sometimes the amount of milk produced at a particular feed does not coincide with the baby's needs at that time.

Expense Breast milk is virtually free. But the breast-feeding mother may need to spend rather more money than usual on her own diet which must be rich in calcium, protein and vitamins.

Convenience Breast milk is instantly available – at the correct temperature and usually sterile. But only the mother can feed the baby, and her health and well-being affect the milk supply. Any medicines or alcohol she takes may affect the infant.

bottle feeding

Quality Formula milks have been developed that are very similar in composition to breast milk. But finding the formula that is most suitable for the needs of a particular infant can be a matter of trial and error.

There is no formula equivalent to colostrum.

Bottle-fed babies are more likely to suffer from nappy rash and more likely to be overweight.

Quantity It is possible to see at a glance how much milk the baby has taken. The quantity of milk offered can easily be adjusted to meet the baby's needs.

Expense Initial expense is involved in purchasing the various pieces of equipment needed for bottle feeding.

Milk formula must be bought over a period of several months.

Convenience Formulas need mixing, and strict sterilization procedures must be followed. These are quite time consuming. The father and other adults can help feed the baby, relieving the burden on the mother.

your baby's food needs

The quantity of milk required by the baby will vary according to his weight and age. In the first few days after his birth, the baby will take tiny feeds at irregular intervals. By about the end of the first week his pattern of feeding will probably have become more regular. From this point food requirements increase fairly steadily and are reflected in a correspondingly steady gain in weight.

It is possible to calculate the baby's approximate daily food needs in ounces by multiplying his weight to the nearest pound by 2½. Each baby's requirements are slightly different and a particular baby's requirements may vary from day to day. The diagram is a guide to the amount of milk required by typical babies at different ages.

Typical feeding requirements

Feed intake
per day
in ounces

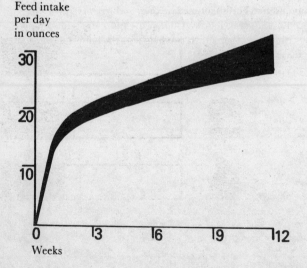

formula milk

A wide range of commercially produced formula milks is now available for bottle-fed babies. Scientific research into the constituents of human and animal milks has enabled manufacturers to produce milk formulas that are well suited to babies' needs. Baby milk formulas are generally made by modifying cow's milk to make it more like human milk. One important change is shown in the diagram – an adjustment to the relative proportions of carbohydrate, protein, and fat. The actual nature of these nutrients is also modified – as are the proportions of different minerals and vitamins.

A very few babies are unable to take milk of any kind – and special non-milk formulas have been developed to meet their needs (see p. 113).

Modification of cow's milk in
milk formula production   Gm per 100ml

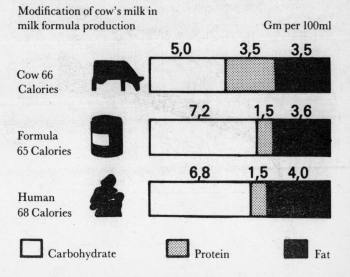

	5,0	3,5	3,5
Cow 66 Calories			
	7,2	1,5	3,6
Formula 65 Calories			
	6,8	1,5	4,0
Human 68 Calories			

□ Carbohydrate   ▦ Protein   ■ Fat

feeding equipment

If the baby is to be bottle-fed, you and your partner should
ensure that all the feeding equipment is ready before the birth.
Even if the baby is to be breast fed, a few bottles and teats for
the occasional supplementary feed or fruit drink will be needed.

1 Six bottles and caps
2 Sterilizing unit and six teats
3 Measuring jug
4 Flat-bladed knife
5 Spoon for adding sugar (if
used)
6 Long-handled mixing
spoon
7 Measuring scoop for
formula
8 Bottle brush
9 Tray for storage

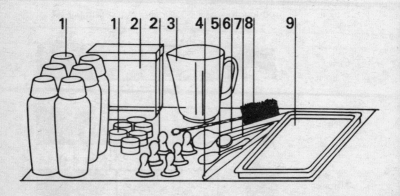

teats

The size of the hole in the teat is extremely important. Teats with large holes are inadvisable for young babies because the milk flows too freely, causing indigestion or choking. Small holes restrict the milk flow but can be enlarged – either with a hot needle held in a cork (**1**), or by using a razor blade to make a cross-cut in the end of the teat (**2**).

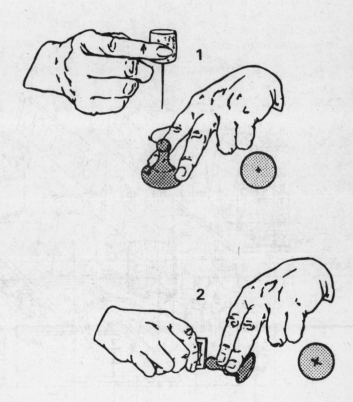

the working area

It is a good idea to keep close together the different items needed for preparing feeds. Most people find it convenient to store equipment and formula in an area of the kitchen where they are near both a sink and a stove, and where there is a flat working surface. Spare formula and items not in regular use are best stored in a cupboard or on a nearby shelf.

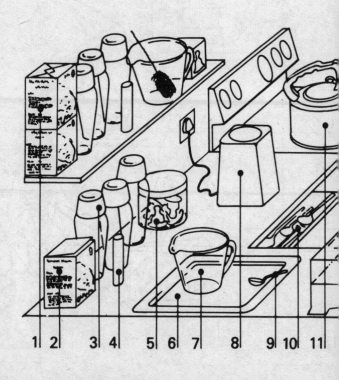

1 2   3 4   5 6 7   8   9 10 11

1 Spare equipment shelf
  Formula
  Bottles
  Sterilizing tablets
  Measuring cup
  Bottle brush
  Teats
2 Formula
3 Bottles
4 Sterilizing tablets
5 Teats in a jar
6 Tray
7 Measuring jug
8 Bottle warmer
9 Scoop
10 Cutlery
11 Kettle
12 Sterilizing unit
13 Sink
14 Bottle brush
15 Hot, soapy water

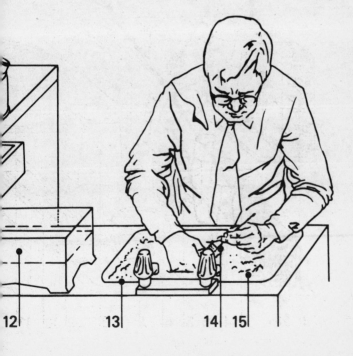

feeding bottles

Feeding bottles are available in a variety of styles. They are
usually made from heat-resistant glass or plastic. A wide-
necked bottle (**1a**) has the advantage of being easy to clean with
a bottle brush (**1b**). But a narrow-necked bottle (**2**) helps
prevent the baby from taking in air with the milk. Small bottles
like (**3**) and (**4**) are useful for using in addition to a breast feed
or for giving water or fruit drinks. The straight-sided bottle (**5**)
is fitted for convenience with disposable, ready-sterilized,
plastic lining sacs.

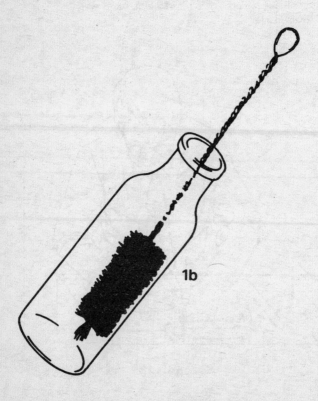

1b

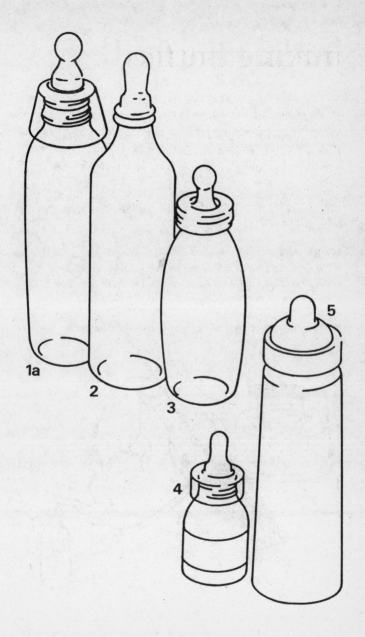

1a

2

3

5

4

mixing the feed

There are two basic types of formula milk – powder and liquid.
Both are made from modified cow's milk and reconstituted
with water for feeding. Some brands are unsuitable for young
babies so it is important to follow the instructions of the
midwife, doctor, health visitor or nurse at your clinic. It is also
wise to seek medical advice before changing from one formula
to another.

WARNING
● Never make a bottle too strong by overloading the scoop or
adding extra formula. Over-concentrated mixture can cause
stomach upsets or even kidney problems and can result in
obesity.
● Never add extra sweetening except on medical advice.

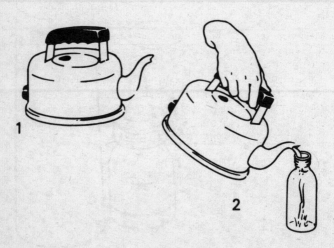

preparing powder formula

1 Check that the baby has a dry nappy; change if necessary. Wash hands. Boil water in a kettle; leave to cool slightly.
2 Pour water into sterilized bottle to half the final feed quantity required.
3 Scoop powder from package into bottle, levelling each scoop with the back of a knife. Count the scoops carefully. Sweetening is added now only if specified in the manufacturer's instructions, or if advised by your doctor.
4 Fix sterilized cap to top of bottle and shake. Remove cap and top up to desired level with cooled, boiled water.
5 Attach sterile teat. Check temperature and rate of flow by shaking a few drops on to the inside of the wrist. The milk must not feel hot and should run in a rapid stream of drops.

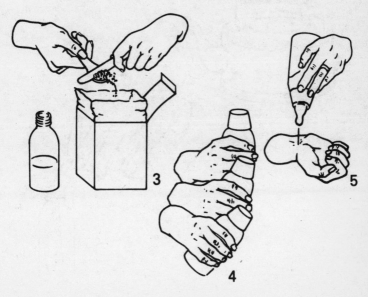

preparing liquid formula

1 Check that the baby has a dry nappy; change if necessary.
Wash hands. Boil water in a kettle; leave to cool slightly.
2 Scrub and scald top of can. Open can and pour prescribed
quantity of formula into a sterilized bottle.
3 Add required amount of cooled, boiled water from kettle.
4 Fix on sterilized cap and shake bottle.
5 Attach sterile teat. Check temperature and rate of flow by
shaking a few drops on to the inside of the wrist. The milk must
not feel hot and should run in a rapid stream of drops.

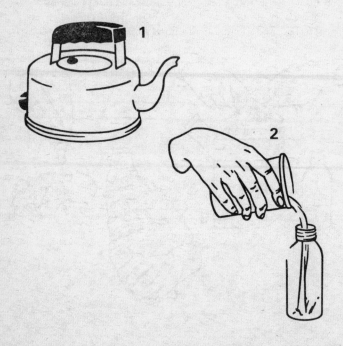

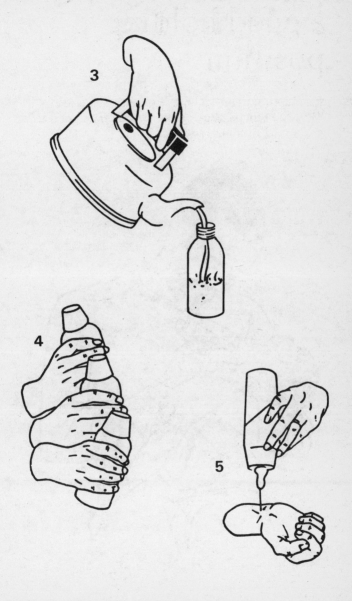

99

a good holding position

Make sure that you and the baby are comfortable before offering the bottle of prepared milk formula. Any milk left at the end of a feed must be discarded.

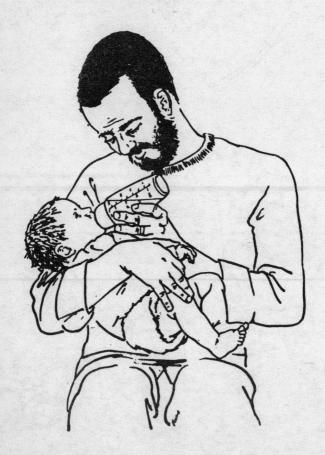

mixing in a measuring jug

Another method of preparing formula is to mix the powder or liquid in a measuring cup before transferring it to the bottle. This is particularly useful for formulas to which sweetening is added, or for formulas that need stirring with a spoon or fork. It is also recommended when preparing several feeds at the same time (p. 102).

Measure the formula for one or more feeds into a large jug and mix it to a paste with a little cooled, boiled water (**1**). Add more cooled, boiled water to bring the feed up to the right amount and pour the formula into one or more bottles (**2**). The feed can be used immediately or stored in the refrigerator for up to 24 hours.

feeds for the day

If you have a refrigerator, it may be simpler to prepare feeds for the whole day. The bottles can be made up one by one (see p. 97) or the entire quantity can first be mixed in a large measuring jug (see p. 101). After making up, the bottles not needed for an immediate feed should be placed in the refrigerator.

Never store made-up bottles for more than 24 hours. When a bottle is required it is not necessary to reheat it; many babies find cold milk quite acceptable. You may, however, prefer to warm the milk. This can be done by standing the bottle in a jug of hot water; by putting the bottle in a saucepan of water while the water is brought to the boil; or by means of an electric bottle warmer.

bottle feeding

It is vital that a bottle-fed baby should not be denied any of the warmth, intimacy, and security that a breast-fed baby enjoys during feeds. To achieve this, the person giving the bottle should make a point of cuddling the baby, holding him securely, and talking to him quietly and lovingly. In this way he will come to associate the pleasure of feeding with the people who love and care for him.

On some occasions it may be tempting to prop a bottle on a folded nappy or use a bottle holder. But this is much less satisfactory from the baby's point of view. Very young babies must never be left alone with a bottle because of the risk of choking. From the age of about six months a baby may be allowed to hold his own bottle under supervision.

It is important to hold the bottle correctly when feeding a baby. If the baby sucks in a lot of air with the milk, the resulting wind in his stomach will cause him discomfort.

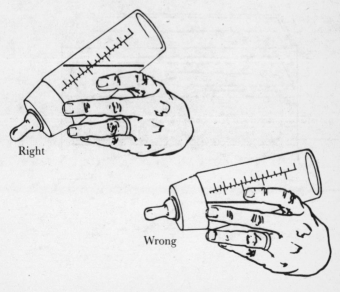

Right

Wrong

aseptic preparation

When using the aseptic method of food preparation, all
equipment is sterilized beforehand and the milk formula is
mixed with cooled, boiled water.
1 All equipment – bottles, teats, spoons, etc. – must be
sterilized before mixing begins. Many people now do this with
commercially produced sterilizing tablets or fluids. These are
added to cold water in a container specially designed to keep
the equipment immersed. It is most important to follow the
manufacturers' instructions when using any of these products.
Alternatively, equipment may be sterilized by boiling for 25
minutes in a sterilizer unit or covered saucepan.

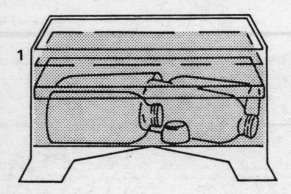

2 The formula is mixed in the bottles, using cooled, boiled water. The equipment should be handled as little as possible. Alternatively, the formula may first be mixed in a measuring jug (see p. 101).

3 Any bottle not intended for immediate use should have the teat inserted in its neck, and should be placed in the refrigerator.

4 Caps should be screwed tightly on all bottles prepared for future use.

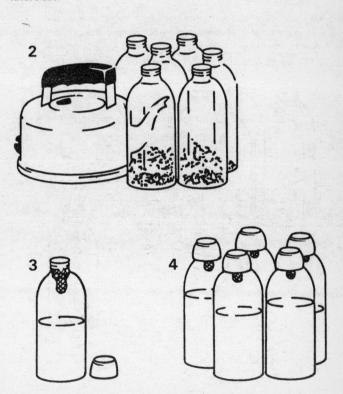

terminal sterilization

In the terminal method of sterilization the prepared milk is sterilized along with the bottles and the teats.

1 Milk formula is measured into the bottles, which have previously been washed but not sterilized. (You should use hot, soapy water and a bottle brush to get the bottles really clean and free from milk deposits. Always rinse the bottles in clean water.)

2 Cold water from the tap is used for mixing the formula.

3 A clean teat is inverted in the neck of the bottle. (Rubbing the teats with a little salt before washing will remove the film of milk which sometimes collects inside them.)

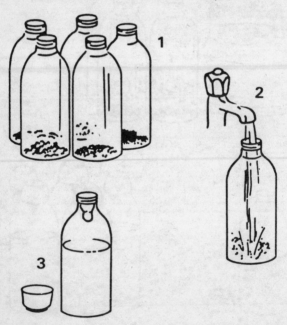

4 The bottle caps are put on – loosely so that the steam can pass under them – and the bottles are placed upright in 3in (8cm) of water in a sterilizer unit or covered saucepan.
5 The water is brought to the boil, and after 25 minutes' boiling the sterilizer should be left to cool for two hours with its lid in place. (Gradual cooling helps to prevent a skin from forming on the surface of the milk.) The bottles are removed from the sterilizer, and those not intended for immediate use should have their caps screwed on tightly before storage in the refrigerator.

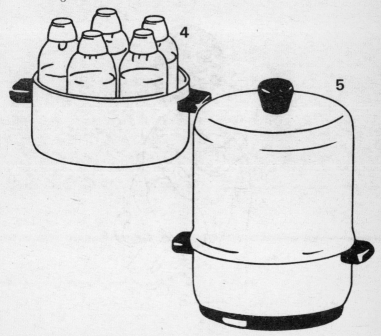

winding the baby

During a feed a baby swallows air which forms a bubble in his stomach. To prevent discomfort, it is important to get up this air bubble at least once during a feed and again at the end. Here are three ways of winding your baby:

1 Hold the baby against your shoulder and gently rub his back.
2 Hold the baby sitting upright in your lap and gently rub his back.
3 Lie the baby across your lap and gently rub his back.

In each case, it is useful to have a cloth to wipe away any milk regurgitated from the baby's mouth.

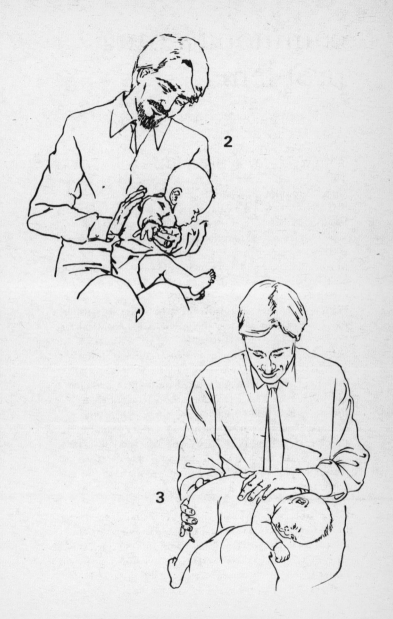

2

3

common feeding problems

Some babies have feeding problems that can cause considerable distress and anxiety to parents.

Very young babies sometimes feed for a very short time and then fall asleep, only to wake a few minutes later for more milk. This can be exhausting and frustrating for everyone, but it is almost certainly only a passing phase. The nervous and digestive systems of some babies do not at first work properly together, so that the baby does not make the connection between sucking and the relief of his hunger. He will soon stay awake long enough to satisfy his hunger.

Meanwhile, you could try changing the baby's feeding position or, if the baby is breast-fed, the mother could try moving him from breast to breast more frequently.

Feeding problems can also arise because babies are sensitive to the moods of those who feed them. This is obviously true for breast-fed babies but is also true in the case of babies who are bottle-fed. If the person giving the feed is tired, rushed, or anxious the baby may sense this and become restless and difficult to feed. A calm and relaxed atmosphere at feeding times should help matters. If there are older children, try to see that the baby is fed in a different room where there is no distracting noise. Perhaps you or your partner could entertain the older child while the baby is being fed; especially in the early days, this is when sibling rivalry can manifest itself in a most unhelpful way! If you can arrange to spend a little time settling the older child before you begin to feed the baby, disturbance is less likely.

Older babies may feed badly if they are teething or suffering from an ear infection which makes jaw movements painful. If discomfort temporarily prevents a baby from sucking, you can try giving formula or expressed breast milk from a small cup or from a spoon. Blocked nasal passages following a cold can make breathing during a feed difficult for the baby. Your doctor may be able to suggest a nasal inhalant or drops that can be used just before a feed to free the passages and make sucking easier.

Bottle-fed babies A bottle-fed baby can lose interest in his feed if the milk does not flow quickly enough through the teat. This can be remedied by enlarging the teat hole as described on p. 91.

Breast-fed babies In the case of a breast-fed baby, problems affecting the mother, such as retracted nipples or engorgement, can mean that the baby has considerable difficulty in taking the areola into his mouth to begin feeding. Occasionally a baby refuses to feed during the mother's menstrual period. This is upsetting for the mother, but she should be encouraged to express her milk to avoid discomfort, and to offer the baby bottled formula milk for a day or two.

feeding premature babies

Feeding a premature baby during the first few days, or even weeks, of life demands the expert attention of trained hospital staff. In a premature infant the control of vital functions such as breathing, sucking and swallowing is restricted and, in many cases, the digestive system is still immature and unable to cope easily with the normal processes of digestion.

One of the major hazards of feeding premature infants is that improperly digested food may be regurgitated and inhaled into the lungs, causing choking.

Most premature babies are not fed until 48 hours after birth. They are fed very small quantities of milk, usually every three hours, from a dropper or by means of a tube passed down the throat into the stomach. The feeding consists of formula milk or breast milk expressed by the mother. When the baby's weight has increased and his ability to suck has improved, he can be fed normally from breast or bottle. The baby will still require very small quantities at frequent intervals.

The premature baby has few nutritional reserves and is often so short of iron that slight anaemia results. This can be corrected by a prescription of medicinal iron from about the fourth week. Vitamin supplements are usually given from the second week.

hiccups and sickness

Many young babies suffer from hiccups after feeds, but they are rarely upset by them. You may find that the hiccups can be stopped by offering a drink of cooled, boiled water, or simply by burping the baby.

Some gentle regurgitation or 'spitting' of milk is quite normal after a feed, particularly during the early months. As long as the baby's weight gain is satisfactory there is rarely anything to worry about.

True vomiting – the ejection of the contents of the stomach with some force – is much less common. It may be the symptom of an infection or obstruction, and cases of persistent vomiting always need medical attention.

milk-allergic babies

A very few babies who fail to thrive are found to be allergic to milk. This allergy is identified by a series of hospital tests, after which the doctor will prescribe a special non-milk formula.

These specially developed milk-free formulas typically contain such ingredients as soya beans, corn and coconut oils, sucrose, and corn sugar. Other formulas have been developed using modified meat protein.

A baby fed on a special non-milk formula can be expected to have normal rates of growth.

colic

Colic is a severe abdominal pain that affects many babies
between the ages of two weeks and three months. Attacks
usually occur daily, often in the evening, and can last up to four
hours.

A baby with colic typically refuses to settle down after the late
afternoon or early evening feed. He begins to scream – often
adopting the position shown.

During an attack the baby can be comforted temporarily by
cuddling him, or wrapping his blankets tightly around him. His
distress returns, however, as soon as he is left again.

The causes of colic are unclear and medical opinion is still in
disagreement. Some doctors suggest some precautions that
might prevent an attack. The baby should not be allowed to
feed too quickly; he should be thoroughly winded after a feed;
and he should be kept warm.

The illustration shows a baby with the characteristic signs of
colic.

- Screaming
- Legs drawn up to the
  stomach
- Tightly clenched fists

weaning and introducing solids

Weaning is the term used for the gradual substitution of solid foods for milk in an infant's diet. Exact schedules and procedures for weaning vary considerably – the advice of your doctor or clinic nurse or health visitor is the best guide for the optimal growth and development of your child.

Typically, weaning begins at about four months, and by 12 months the infant should be taking a wide variety of solid foods.

Phasing out milk feeds During the first stages of weaning the infant continues to receive five breast or bottle feeds daily, but the amount of milk is reduced at any feed at which solids are also offered. From about six months, you can safely give your child undiluted cow's milk in place of breast or formula milk. Milk and milk products remain an important part of diet throughout childhood.

Traditionally the first solid food offered to an infant consists of cereal or rusk mixed to a creamy consistency with milk. However, it is quite acceptable to start weaning with a little pureed apple or a small amount of proprietary baby food. Whichever solid food is chosen, it is first given at one feed daily and is given in addition to breast or formula milk. After a week or two solids are given at two feeds, and after a few more weeks the infant should be given a variety of different solid foods at three feeds each day.

Gradually the infant's food pattern becomes more like that of the rest of the family – with three meals a day and drinks on waking and at bedtime.

weaning equipment

From the time your baby first begins to take solid food a considerable variety of equipment will be needed at mealtimes. Learning to eat is always a messy process – especially when the baby first starts to feed himself. For this reason, it is advisable to have towelling or plastic bibs to protect clothing and easy-wipe surfaces or mats to protect furniture. Some feeds may be given on your lap, but the baby will need a rigid seat with a table when he begins to feed himself. Many baby chairs can be used also as a low chair or fitted on to a stand for use as a high chair. Cups and dishes should be unbreakable and designed for easy use. Cutlery should be small enough for the baby to handle.

1 Angled spoon
2 Small spoon
3 Small fork
4 Plastic mat
5 Double-handed cup with spout
6 Beaker with spout

7 Plastic bib with trough
8 Towelling bib
9 Heavy-based dish with straight sides for easy use
10 Double dish with hollow base for hot water to keep food warm

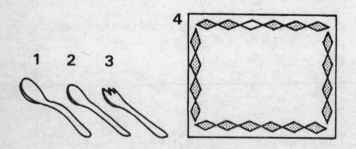

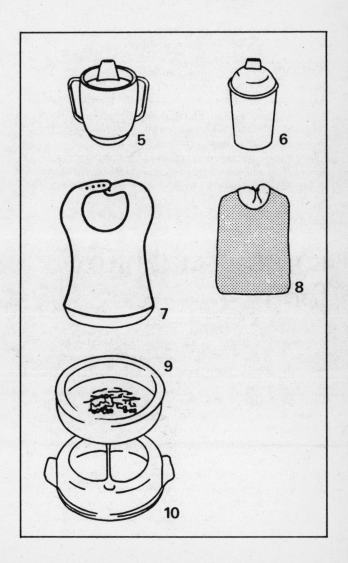

feeding procedures

In the early stages of weaning, small tastes of solid food should be given on a teaspoon. Place the spoon in the baby's mouth so that he can suck the food from it. At the first few feeds, it is often worth offering the milk before the solid food so that the baby's acute hunger has been satisfied. The baby should be encouraged to drink from a cup.

After a few months the baby will probably want to pick up food in his fingers and show signs of wanting to feed himself from a spoon. This is the start of a lengthy and messy process but it is important to let your baby persevere. Feeding can be speeded up if you slip an occasional spoonful of food into the baby's mouth when he becomes tired or fretful.

commercial baby foods

It is often convenient to use commercial baby foods, and manufacturers have undertaken a great deal of research recently to produce foods to match the nutritional needs of babies and toddlers.

There are two basic types – ready to serve in cans or jars, and powdered foods for mixing with milk or water. Ranges include foods suitable for the early stages of weaning – broths, and purees of fruit, vegetables, and meat – and a great variety of foods for the slightly older child.

Particularly in the early stages of weaning, powdered foods can prove the most economical as tiny quantities can be prepared without affecting the quality of the remainder of the package. Food from a can or jar, once opened, can be stored for a short time provided that certain precautions are observed (see p.120).

home-prepared foods

With a little time and trouble many items from your family's diet can be adapted to suit your baby's needs. Food for a young baby must be in puree form, so a sieve, food mill, or blender are essential. As the baby becomes accustomed to solids, mashing, mincing, or chopping are usually sufficient. Too much salt or sugar is harmful to babies, so seasoning should be kept to a minimum.

Vegetables – particularly cooked carrots, tomatoes, peas, string beans, and potatoes – are good weaning foods. If they are offered one at a time, the baby's preferences can be easily identified.

Egg yolk is a valuable source of iron and can be first introduced mixed with a little cereal. Egg white should not be offered until the baby is at least 9 months old.

Meat broth can be used as an early weaning food and the tasty juices from roast meat can be mixed with mashed vegetables. Beef, lamb, chicken, and liver – pureed or minced – are all suitable for the slightly older baby.

Non-oily fish can be served if all the bones are removed.

Cheese is another nourishing weaning food. Grated cheese can be mixed with cereal as an alternative to sweetening. Later many babies like to hold and chew on a piece of cheese.

Firm foods should be given to babies to encourage chewing and teething. Suitable foods include raw carrot and apple, small pieces of toast, and crusts of bread.

using commercial foods

Small quantities of baby food can be heated in a cup over very hot water. The food can then be fed directly from the cup or it can be transferred to a dish. If the baby has not been fed directly from the jar or can, and if it has not been heated up, any remaining food can be stored, covered, in the refrigerator for up to two days.

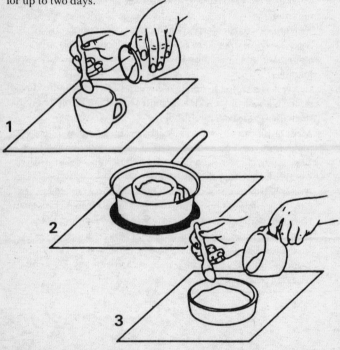

1 Place sufficient food for one meal in a cup
2 Heat by placing the cup in hot water
3 Transfer food to a dish for serving

eating sensibly

It is most important to establish sensible eating habits in your child. This is not always easy and can be a cause of some anxiety to concerned parents.

Among the most common problems are: refusal to eat a particular food; refusal to eat properly at family mealtimes; and a preference for sweet foods and snacks.

Refusing to eat is rarely serious and parental anxiety will only communicate itself to the child and compound the problem.

Food should be presented as attractively as possible and removed after a certain time without fuss if the child refuses to eat it.

Biscuits, cake, and sweets should only be offered at the end of a meal. Recommended snacks include fresh fruit, fruit juices, and small amounts of cheese.

baby food ingredients

Details of the contents of three popular varieties of canned baby food are given here as an indication of the wide range of commercially produced baby foods.

Beef and carrot casserole
Contents: beef, carrots, potatoes, tomatoes, flour, soya flour, cornflour, herbs, hydrolyzed vegetable protein, iron sulphate.

Calories: 80

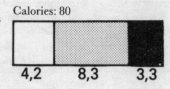

4,2   8,3   3,3

Egg and cheese
Contents: eggs, milk, cheese, semolina, modified cornstarch, vegetable oil, spice.

Calories: 88

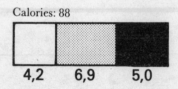

4,2   6,9   5,0

Banana dessert
Contents: banana, sugar, modified cornflour, orange juice, lemon juice, vitamin C.

Calories: 77

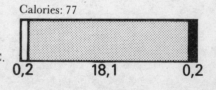

0,2   18,1   0,2

 Protein   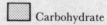 Carbohydrate   Fat

daily food guide

A properly balanced diet is essential for the health and
well-being of even the youngest child. Assessing whether your
child's food needs are being met, however, can be confusing
and difficult. A simple means of checking is to use the daily
food guide shown here.

Devised by a dietician, the guide divides foods into four groups:
1 milk, cheese, and yogurt;
2 fruit and vegetables;
3 meat, fish, and eggs;
4 cereals and bread.

It is recommended that two helpings from each group should
be served every day if possible.

Children suffering from certain illnesses such as diabetes need
diets specially planned under medical supervision.

1 Milk group
Contains protein, carbohydrate, fat, calcium, vitamin A
2 Vegetable and fruit group
Contains carbohydrate, minerals, vitamins A and C
3 Meat, fish, and egg group
Contains protein, fat, iron, vitamins A, B and C
4 Cereals and bread group
Contains protein, carbohydrate, calcium, iron, vitamin B

Index